QUARTETTSATZ

NED CONDINI

BORDIGHERA
WEST LAFAYETTE IN

Library of Congress Cataloging-in-Publication Data

Condini, Ned, 1940-
   Quartettsatz / Ned Condini.
      p.   cm. — (VIA folios ; 7)
   Poems.
   ISBN 1-884419-06-2 (alk. paper)
   I. Title. II. Series.
PS3553.04868Q37   1996
811 '.54—dc20   96-418808
                                   CIP

Printed in the United States.

Published by
BORDIGHERA INCORPORATED
Purdue University
1359 Stanley Coulter Hall
West Lafayette, IN 47907-1359

VIA FOLIOS 7
ISBN 1-884419-06-2

to Marilyn, again . . .
pitch of this music

ACKNOWLEDGMENTS

"Juliet of the Spirits" and "Montvale" first appeared in the collection *Rimbaud in Umbria* (Venice: Multigraf, 1993). "A Notice Arrives Telling Us" was published in the journal *Italian Americana* (University of Rhode Island, 1995).

A section of the title poem, *quartettsatz*, received the 1995 Gozzano Award, Novara, Italy.

TABLE OF CONTENTS

quartettsatz

TENSING THE BOW

Don't offer me wine, my friends; it would sap my strength.
And I'd be ashamed to pour a cup to God
with unwashed hands: I feel splattered with filth.
Let me prepare for this task, scrape off the scurf

on my body, make myself more worthy
to invoke our Lord of joy—He'll set me ablaze,
my daring rhythms flaming with tireless fire.
Then will I drink and, roused by you, win glory.

THE GRAND TETONS

"Split the stone in my forehead,
don't leave me
to my ingrained sterility.

When did she ever sing this song? I don't
recall. But memory finds words,
draws lyrics from its vast profundity."

OVERTURE

Exiled by choice, he coined
a language all his own—
a goblin language, Tetoncha,
to swap for the one foresworn.

A hermit-god he sighted
in the arboreal silence
of the Wyoming mountains
taught it to him, provided

he wrote each word in blood.
A task for an immortal.
Irked by his verse, the royal
critics drew back in dread.

So he read it to a few friends
and the creatures of the forest.
After reading each quatrain
he consigned it to the flame.

Nobody knew of the burning
but his friends and the beasts.
They were so enthused by poetry
that they forgot to eat.

They just listened. The king's
men who hunted them down
found them terribly thin.
Soon at the palace the butchers

were at a loss: no good meat
for the courtly table. The Throne
decided 'twas time to atone.
Shamefacedly, he called the poet

back to his reign, changed his fate,
begged him recite his lines
at the lavish banquet. Too late.
Most lovely songs were gone,

burned. All that he could get
was a sample of what was left.

LIFE IS A BITCH, & THEN

you die, the truck license hooted.
Life is a beach, we tooted,
from where we watch the sea.
That blue, so charmingly reachable,
those waves, so mighty and affable—
leaning to hear our plea.

So, stranded on the sand,
we sifted its gold through our fingers,
thinking to prop a dyke
against the flow: grim poverty,
time burned on fame and study,
the lost, unsullied loves
and our loveless families—
the gory horrors of youth.

Then, even gold lost its luster.
From the ocean's secret grottoes
needles popped up, oil oozed,
muck of man's screwed up legacy.
Yet the blue strangely stayed,
at least from afar, immaculate,
but once touched with our old
exhausted limbs, how cold
& vicious. The horrors of age,
our fury at the unbroken bar,

the blue face of God receding,
our loss of hope, evil star.

VASSAR COLLEGE

Branches there are alive with wings,
each house a berry glowing
in the crisp October air.

I'd like to go back to Sproul Hall,
its spires, the college nest
safe in a niche of leaves.

On aisles of pines shines
the stained-glass chapel of Vassar
and clouds in amaranth stoles
forgive all escapes, even mine.

I'd like to go back to Sproul Hall,
its clearings, its pubs pulsating
with laughter and smoke, to knowledge
beaten like music on the heart.

A WOMAN'S THOUGHTS

He can watch nature throbbing,
robins heralding spring,
and in the fields an exultation of larks.
But all is no longer as before.

God doesn't see him, hear
his hopes dashed, doesn't care
if he goes back to where he once belonged.
This is the winter of his mind:

shrill is the birds' song in the morning,
chilly on the bones the touch of dew.

HIS ANSWER

True, my dear friend. Explorable and wild
the world appeared to me who contemplated
it with an alien's eye.

And ten years later life is tugging on this side.
The genial face of the sun is different:
it shoots forth megaflames, just as snow
makes a graveyard of all things Here.

Among tornadoes, hurricanes and floods,
under a sweeping sky that's charged
with black clouds at its mildest,
that breathes its rowdy slang
of rough landscapes and men—
I accept to be who I am
and with whom and where.
An American who cannot despair.

NOW THE MUSE SPEAKS

You're not by chance another Trofimovic,
or do you really think that in high circles
people watch you all the time, counting your steps,
and the red mayor has enquired
of you right after the elections?
Don't feel sore—you've got nothing to fear;
nor is it true that you are persecuted,
that "they" all want to have you ostracized.
Simply, between us, we would like to get
some explanations. Instead you take off
and wear an exile's suffering air.

Nobody has banned you, and nobody hates you.
It's even worse: nobody gives a damn.
Ah, Stepàn: dismal times
begin right now.

A NOTICE ARRIVES TELLING US
YOU'VE WON A GRANT FROM WYOMING

Forgive me, if on nagging days of loss—
when your hands stiffen, drained of lymph, or floods
of heat batter your chest—if I have heart
and cannot snap the threads of love that hold me
tied to a world of flesh and blood.

A lulling breeze seduces me, the smell
of wet cut grass, an iridescent moon
astride the trees, the boom of distant thunder,
a sudden hush in the forsythia—wonders.

Nocturnal warmths of spring are in the air,
echoing our eager youth, a rare
marriage of constellations in the sky.
This aged wine burns, and I want you to drink it
with me, feel it rush down your thirsty throat,
and mesmerized, on desolating days
of loss, forget for this glory your cross.

JACKSON HOLE

He does not miss the shade of carob trees,
the palm stretching its branches to survive,
the prickly pear shielding its fruit with thorns.
He comes from the North & the granite of mountains.
Bouquet of spruce is on his breath & freshness
of icy streams. Ghosts come to him & whisper
tales of the dead from their high latitudes.

He nestles in crystal air, sees things in their nakedness.
No saffron, violet, damask to entice
his steady heart into the South's wild flames.

SAINT FRANCIS CHAPEL, DUBOIS

In this dark Advent when
no resurrection's seen
nor His lamb heard bleating peace to the world,
I send you only what a son's contrition
can send to a deceased father: love and rest,
freedom at last, absorbed into the sun
the long fever of his day.

COMPARING BROTHERS

The gent with the proper accent
(strangers sum him up)
and a face somewhat foreign, as if Europe had molded
his features too fine, tempered the Yankee zest
for the tough but true.

His friends, though, know fierce love
brought him here and a lion's rage
for climbing each day, in the 'good old country,'
someone else's stairs, eating their stale, dry bread.
He booted the Boot, they say, for whatever stung

small and unfair in that uncivil land
of fractious barons, chose *Hud*
over *Tears in The Band.*
Yet when nostalgia for his snow-capped Alps
grips him, his passion

for sights clean and smooth,
and he trudges back to that vivid stretch of acres
gold and green in the valley of his youth,
at the Matterhorn's base, 'The American,'
they say. His Italian's native.

Is it his grin that betrays him, the habit he has
of standing tall, recalling deep-flowing rivers,
towering crags, strength drunk from boundless horizons:
he walks and talks like an American now.
He faces his mountains with an American mind.

TAKING LEAVE

At times I wish I could fall asleep in the snow.
Soft flakes would cover me and in that white from heaven
winter would just be a blanket tucking me in.
Or do I crave green, trees caroling with buds,
Hawaiian bays, spring winging back again . . .
At times I see myself strolling by the ocean,
the pounding surf a stirring symphony
of sun-drenched thoughts flavored with salt. But soon
autumn wades in with its grand cadences,
hints on the wind that frost is here
even if maples point to scarlet heights
the weary heart cannot reach as before.
I wish my death were a blending of seasons—
all the world's colors alchemied to light.

MUSPELHEIM

The blank page sits before me
stubborn and bare: Christ's dead,
dead too my father, and I with him,
in absolute indifference.
His end still doesn't move me
nor his life warm me enough to make me cross
this ocean, go visit his tomb.

Did that dust ever like me?
Before I left, what did he say about me?
Questions that have no answers
just like the graveyard: it won't speak,
and yet I want to recollect today.

Is it true he repented
surrendering to the mean disease
or did Mother think up, unwittingly,
the guileless fib?
        How do you talk to a phrenastenic,
what do you say to God, and who is He?
Because if He does not exist we'd better
strangle the world—until all humans croak.

This going under: will it ever end.
I so would like to say I love you, but I can't.
I wish you would have said it,
but not with a face ravaged by pain.
A flood besieges me of all missed opportunities,
cowardly moments, all the honest things
I could have spun around the axis of my life
without hurting, without humiliating,
without having to say too many times:
I didn't mean it.

JULIET OF THE SPIRITS

The priest is hissing murky
instructions to the nuns: the pyre is ready,
winch up Giulietta, let her more triumphant
burn in her martyrdom.
                              Bellies to the ground,
the crows cross themselves cawing
the *miserere* of death, from tongues of fire
my life of terror leaps. Sin everywhere,
bending flowers display
inviting sexes, statues move their naked
parts bawdily, awnings jut out or widen,
from those who walk clothes are torn off, and flesh
desecrated flares up. The world is lewd.

. . . Who kicks the hot coals of the brothel,
pulls the priest by his beard, stifles the stench
of sulphur, cuts the ties and frees Juliet
from the flames?
                              The fire now laps friendly,
flowers unglue their bills, statues resume
innocent poses, satyrs go after love
without their cloven hoofs, the baldachin
raised on my sacrifice and treason
founders submerged in an ocean of white.

MANATEE

1

A little light bobs and flares
with fragile diminutive wings.
Shine in the dark, firefly
afraid of not being seen.

I remember we would sit
together in the meadow.
Evening would come. "Which of us,"
you asked, "will live longer?"

Looking at grass and flowers
we felt like giants;
now roots play between your eyes
& sod weighs on your breast
to keep your heart still.

Waters run to the sea, the clouds fly,
the leaves walk with the wind.
Only you don't move. I thought everything
lived just for you.

2

In my dreams you materialize
as from submarine kingdoms,
your flippers busy sorting
the succulent weeds;
you swim near in full confidence,
your mouth takes from my hands
bunches of tendrils pulled out just for you.

But someone stronger ensnares
and hooks to nets without exit
a helpless guinea pig,
your flesh drilled by harpoons.

Dear, throughout Florida
the gentle manatee is hunted and killed.
His innocence condemns him.

3

I wanted to apologize to you,
thank you for all your favors,
praise your courage at least one time . . .
but earlier, when the wounds on your face
were veils still, the unruly curl
before you lost it, amber.

Geraniums will live without you,
no son will drive you up a wall
nor finicky husband redress
the awesome disorder of your rooms.

Out of joint it is we now who howl.
What remains: a whisper
to stagger back to, your name on a tomb.

4

Red hearts are beating
in the field by your townhouse,
birds by the thousands . . . lean
from your terrace up there,
let down your long hair,

the hem of your skirt! to pull me
wherever you are. And I'll up
and go without looking back once.

LONDON BROIL

Adolescent mornings, the vigils
so fervid! The lamp's yellow halo
on the table a circumference of thought
and clarity in the unbroken silence—
when I read Webster out loud
and in a filthy boarding house
declaimed thousands of lines
fixed in my search like Hieronimus.

Afternoons with dreary rain falling
on a tea-less suburban dust hole
of London, the landlady every so often
leering on the threshold, orutund,
nymphomaniacal: could she make the bed?
I got it after she'd already gone.

All then was light of learning, chastity.
Later, night fright, obsolete
broken syllables on graveyard slabs.
We felt like burning the world.
Riots at school, the science sub assaulted,
King and Kennedy murdered, Father moaning
in hospitals, poor Mother all but loony.

Sweating it out at Berkeley, later at Vassar
teaching rich girls *Death's Duel*, e.e. cummings'
cutesy lyrical puns:
uncertainties, presages of greatness
mostly in the bathroom, repentances, vile thoughts,
De Sade's longings and from each ridge and gorge
His booming voice to scare me in the corner.

COMRADES, À NOUS!

"Rightist or Leftist?"—undecided for a moment,
the wrong answer, and they wouldn't let you through,
would slap or push you, hit you with a chain.

The "lucha" was in progress. In neo-Fascist
uniforms or dressed à la Ho Chi Min
they wanted all things Now.

Wildmother Turin, jelly-like ectoplasm
run over day and night by paranoids
in marines' jackets, in brown shirts (or red ones),
by artists of the Bomb.

I left the mongrel city far behind.
I left behind, remorseless, just the blue
of my Rócciamelóné peak,
Ulzio's 'boleti' and the Col del Lys
teeming with daffodils in April.

UPDIKE AT REST

The swift of pace dash by on cheetah's paws,
linger a moment, see his cautious smile
open up like a flower, then run miles

to tap strange myths, uncover new domains.
But he aches for the company of old friends—
the tall oaks in the yard, the jays' shrill screech.

A puff-ball rabbit sits upon the grass
as if made out of cedar. He won't barter
these for any race now, nor polished speech.

At last we met
like hawks meet in air,
in a blue space, and now I think the world
won't stay with us long enough,
I won't have time to learn
all the seasons you wear.

You're a song I could sing forever,
but death's a road
that mountains interrupt
without subtracting
from the invisible distance.

ARIEL ARISES

My feet wear petrel's wings:
green and blue, from a thin
trickle of foam they draw
numberless brackish melodies.

As I run on wet sand
I transcribe liquid timbers,
link in my fleeting passage
chords and the pause that lingers.

From on high, an odd whiteness
is spreading on the shores:
halcyons have laid their eggs
with sharks and albacores.

Mellow September, flutist
of orchards, eyes mauve moons,
clears the sky modulating
a consonance with bones.

No whitecaps rear, no whirlpool
gurgles, no swooshing's heard—
the dunes bask in the blissful
air like a sleeping herd.

Deep down in every substance
light lies and silence swells.
Already, autumn equinox,
I feel your honeyed spell.

On the lazy sea devoid
of sails the charm's suspended:
supine in the amassed gold
of leaves summer is ended.

MONTVALE
(for Alan Brent)

Throughout the woods the brights
sever the road from silence
our relaxing bodies
from an animal's quiver
words (where & if they reach us)
are clipped to suit the weather of the valley

we would like to be strong
but darkness is so sweet
the thoughts between us
flow so perfectly attuned
that we run a hare's track
or wear moss on our hearts

& from our legs leaves sprout
the river invades our blood
the sky pounces on us
for the sadness of all
we are & will never be
for days gone up in smoke

II

MUSPELHEIM

1

In his bed, as he was talking of everything
and nothing, his calm made me shiver.
I walked around the sun-bleached avenues
of the hospital, ashamed of myself,
of his sickness, of my frivolity,
beyond worried urban faces
that shunned me, closed in their enmity.

Dad, you were awful: I wanted to rub
every single scar on your skin;
you were unfair: I wanted to break
every single bone in your body.

2

I finished him off. Remorse, pressing,
produces Dad's emaciated chest,
the ramblings of the final months.

If I shed his blood, from now on
every word of mine takes on its color.
The first turning point is language,
the first move from cowardice to courage.

3

What do you mean: I don't remember you?
With me goes the bookcase you made,
board by board, from ocean to ocean;
your crumpled photo lies in my breast pocket.
Or did the sentence that slipped out
of my mouth one day, calling selfish
the gift of your whole life, part us?
At the crossing of Martyrs' Street
and the Sports Center I wait
with a glassful of wine: you might
come back to me thirsty.

4

"The encrusted eyes useless before evening,
the heavy head already stunned at noon.
The whole day sitting, shutters drawn,
or leaning on a cane.

I give off smells, my beard is stubbly, I come
and go only for corporal needs.
Fewer and fewer my contacts with the world,
more inexplicable the wish to be
closer to her, mute, forbearing. Not alone!"

5

Gods do lead men in dreams.
Sunk in sleep on the parvis
of a church in Mahwah,
a parvis of red leaves,
a shape of light stood up before me
with a golden reed in its hand.
With this, it said, you will find your father.

So here I am trekking towards your ranges
with a wrenching need for oxygen.
I plod along the steep grass
sliding, falling, no markers in sight.
The way to the pass winds through
a rumble of avalanches.

6

"Can it be that if the mind goes backwards
the body too resumes its former state?
and that between body and soul
the body weakens and the soul stays stronger?
Because by day my paralyzed feet falter,
by night they jump over valleys."

7

It can be. You never awoke
to see a mourning son bent over you.

I was there, father, though too late,
and only in a dream.

8

The unknown figure before me climbs
ethereally, an inner concentration
lifting it off the ground.
Walking fast to keep out the cold
we meet the dying sun where
one more canyon widens.
Camped in a cave, eating slowly
we watch the mountains put out stars.

A shade flits by, not he, but like him
in tesserae of coals . . . Would it were possible
to see him only for a little while,
to know what he is now—blessed or in fire.

In the morning it's windy, all is frozen,
and snow has fallen.
On these slopes where my father was born
I feel open and clean. The two hands I see
before me in the sun—browned, skinned by life—
are exactly like his.

BIVOUAC

April, and I have traveled half the world,
seen loads of people, not counting the dead
whom perhaps I was calling when (benumbed
by cold and cramped in my stiff sleeping bag,
bowie-knife at my belt) marvelous fires
glared off the Chisos.
                        Redux to ETSU,
I write nourishing essays for my chief,
mythologize, commune with resurrected
scholars and martyrs: Münzer, Zwingli, Plato,
Calvin & Huss (sort of nemesis, I,
of the interred ones, bastion of the defeated,
relentlessly fanatic).
                        The last song
of the *Comedy* rags me: How unlike him!
Ambiguous, a lecher masking teases
in sighs, sweating if Susan just by crossing
her legs annihilates my trinitary fits.
Ignoble itches. Always racing to fight,
a non-believer, in your holy name,
stumbling forever, arriving at the scene
of the real combat, never.

OYA TA FULLA

The ground is strewn with tòpazes. He smells
like a leaf ready to be burned and rise,
an offering, to the azure vault of air.
Suddenly a gust of wind, a scarlet flash
of tanagers, a clash of brandished spears,
a roar, a voice freezing the opposing armies
on his backyard turned into a Trojan field.

"Pity the ones whose sons stand up to me!
But if you are an immortal come from heaven,
I'm not the fool to fight the deathless gods."
Undaunted Glaucus leaps down from his chariot,
flawless he faces invincible Diomédes,
warms with astounding tales the soldiers' hearts
fluttering before battle & the kill.

"Like the generations of leaves, the lives of men.
Now the wind scatters old leaves across the earth,
now stumps & boles explode bewitching flowers.
I am Hippólochos' son, son of Bellérophon,
he who slew the Chimaera."
                              "So you're my friend!
My kin hosted Bellérophon, now you be my guest.
Let us trade armor. All here must know our claim."

As if right out of the flaming wings of birds
that generous pause is a song in his ears.
More fervently he rakes the crooning leaves,
(Mother is sick & dying, oya ta fulla)
presses them down in bags with utmost care
to keep them warm in their wait for the Hauler.

III

quartettsatz

(A poem in four voices, male & female, patterned after Schubert's *quartettsatz* and John Berryman's *Delusions*, 1972. Henry is this author's father's name & suicidal American poet John Berryman's nickname. The lines paraphrased from Berryman are 58.)

when the leaf in autumn
loses all its blood,
drunk, drenched with rain,
late with a coin at your window I'll tap.
And in the dripping autumn
when the sky's screaming
even to the dead,
at your window, in the horror of the night,
I'll repeat years go by
more & more brutal.
The rain will patter and I . . .

       so let the world burn! Why
       should one as talented as I
       die? God throw another jerk
       into a hole, not me

only with the wind's hand
will I stroke his hair,
kisses will remain wishes,
marble-lipped statue

       To change evil to good, mend our ways,
       be grateful for the experience;
       to believe that one way or another
       we'll profit from our penance.
       His bounty will rainbow us
       with truth, we'll die transhumanized—

       not the rule. According to data

someone was fooling around
with the elevator. He ran up on foot
and knocked on the door. What cries.
He opened the door and went in.

Can you tell the Judge what you saw?
The woman with a child clasped to her breast.
It looked as if she were hugging him.
They made the noise heard below.
On the bed, smoking, was the man.

The child wailed, clutching the woman,
with her big paws she banged him
against the wall. There were red
stains on her knotty legs.

Down to copulate, up to kill.
Some weep afterwards.
Others, not even that

        His high commands have reached me even here:
        to love my enemies as I love myself.
        Or worse: to love You with my entire mind.

        . . . Perhaps it is not His voice, but only Christ's.
        If you ask man to strive more than he can,
        you're unfair, Lord.

Henry lingered, appalled by all the dead.
The hoary horde waits. Come down!
Unrevealed, monstrous, Protean lull
called existence: this, us.

In a clinic I heard an old man
fed on tubes, doubled over
(for fifteen years not one sensible phrase,
enough to break your heart)
mumble: Come down.

Plain whom he meant.

        You could not bear growing old, but we do.
        Our variances increase.
        The skin is taut or flabby: it does change.
        Reserved, the soul expands by disappearing.
        We awake & stumble on, all in all wiser,
        not more precise.

end of the slaughter
among ruins stands unveiled
the naïve effort to remake the world:
silence, sterile and sodden

I will sit by a corpse in the graveyard
the sealed lips of your father
and mine filling our hearts
with beauty and shivers

> I never saw him again but often ask
> myself whether we'll ever meet by chance
> & soon in twilight's trope
> brushing upon each other—Vedder's herms.
> Will he pause & say, "What is your name?"
> and will I answer, "Who knows, I died last night"?

Curtain curtain on a
puny disgusting life
fable
darkens
the wood
where a birds' trill
still quavered
only silence & centuries
since I from her
departed

Albeit occult at times a soothing voice
here in the air where I lie weak, forlorn
as if it had a body craves to speak
I must go back she misses me
sound that is carried over
feeble feebler a semblance
a
pinpoint
glimmer

> While, kneeling, I was rapt
> in a midnight's grand mystery
> (must, must curtail my evil
> to a minimum I said,

crawling out of my stupor)
I heard again with terror:
'Behold the King's son, cowering,
ragged, unfit to inherit.
Nothing extant of me
but a skull, feet, & rent
among their dogs the palms of my hands.'

Then towers, traffic through jarring chasms, shots,
revolts, Jesus untouched
by stunning whores' catcalls.
Facts, visions . . . yet an ecstasy
of the Afterlife, here, now,
in a child's heart, not difficult to get
but clear as water poured
on bowed brows, dusty sores

is art the word or it translated
as best as one can? Is art more
than the Word? I pore over martyrs
you held high, with a strange wish for pyres.

Levites of eternity! How long?. . .
The dove mourns then dives into the sky.
And of course we misunderstood;
but was what we heard hastened
in the act of memory, or kindled,
or constrained? We implore
for the fingers & tongue to freeze what beauty
suddenly burgeons and stands still

Her beauty nicked by insults,
gray marks on her wrist, pink patches
on her forehead, the scar on her belly—
this the balance for having enjoyed
lips and hands, belly and arms, eyes, a face?
For each orgasm that shook our backs
with tremors, blemishes stuck to the skin,
etched with blotches and lines the strenuous
pleasures of love. I unleafed her
down to her essence. What's left
stares at us: two, alone with death.

At times I think luck
favors constance in deeds of love.
We sighed for years—& yet to each his own!
Bodiless and for nothing we imagine
& make, we makers. In a little while
we will return our fancy tools.
Crude time will burn most of our endeavors

drain, strike, belittle me
but remain as you are
I love the ravings of your sadness your
refusal to be pleased

I glory in you, in your name
in what you are not what you write
unique to me, black spiral in the sun.
Thresh me like corn and I'll give you bread,
press me and I'll be your wine,
bury me and I'll sprout
up from the earth to kiss you in greener leaves

Knowing me was like having
acres of land in Gehènna: Angela, Carol,
Susan, the erotic letters
sent to break down brittle defences

then came marriage and want of *their* bodies
hatred of mine
until a foul smell emanates
all around and it's *me*.

white rabbit
in the tapestry at Arras
hill draped in gold and blue
in Lorenzetti's countryside
your sorrow at the foot
of the Pierced One by van der Weyden

Or are you the rosebush virgin,
the blond queen meeting her saint in armor?

Transfiguration, Miracles
(for me the Crucifixion)
& other creeds solemn and primitive,
modern & dated I studied: fake divinities,
heavenly ones, impotent ones, the power
& malice of the interred

We will all die & afterwards
nada. My love, we do not reunite.
In the meantime be steady & generous

on the screen the last hug is encased
perfectly, its message all too stark.
Or in a novel you read the final scene,
words that ring true, the heart that soars

It's not like that. Incessantly I rehearse
our last confrontation
hoping you will not leave me.

night is an echo to humble lamentations
while I come back home late & tired with fever
removed from you, nearing
the one I wanted to keep out,
towards whom up to now I have been sailing

but the ship careens, doldrums, instructions
squeal from the quarterdeck, the crew is glum,
a hand has morsed: "It's the end."
The Captain is stapling a false log
to a swaying table. Passionate lies sing
in the return trip's cabin. Fires ascend

let speed be held
time be reassessed
not a haphazard race
through nightmares into oblivion

that great thought rather self-
restraint the speech of angels

it can't go on like this there must be

a quick, peaceful demise,
solid as hemlock in that Attic prose
& alive around mé understanding friends

On such a day, when all the hills turn ruby,
light blinds and melts you, shapes you whole,
radiant swells grapes, flames in raspberry briers.
A pup friendly to all, you tear and bite
life from the fields, become a leaf, a river,
a barking song, a vineyard catching fire.

But the embers cool, later you dream

       "No one in!"
               In the middle of the street
       the village madman
       flagged his arms like a wall—
       as if just that was all
       needed to block
       the sudden onset of the night.

Say you lacked nerve, admit weensy
flaws in the Kohinoor's glow.
The pith of your swing calls for glosses—
the poet's freedom, his penchant
unique and distinctive for hell.

I have searched for you far and wide,
Mr. Bones. Where are you hiding,
joined at last with Father? Come out,
greet the dawn! Grace-full and mellow
it's waiting for you as you wanted it:
Empson praising, all enemies lambs.
Not the peace of the hemlock, Henry.

       nowhere. Nowhere. The thing, then, all preset?
       I talk of what I don't get.
       Is God good when He treats his creatures like this?
       Perhaps, O Majesty of the measureless galaxies,
       You might down here one more time overlook

an impenitent Henry?
He studied Your word, & it scared him.

. . . at least strengthen his heart
so that he may endure; soften the first,
the second blows. I can't
believe that You will rack him.

Make the passage easier for my father,
spread over him the fairness of your day.

HEOROT

You get there through danger,
a bog thick with loathsome snakes,
and the murk warns that you
will die in the quest.

Better be brave and steadfast
for trails of blood on the mire
and bits of people It ate
mean that the Beast is near.

Dodging rats big as dogs,
bats with wings like coffin-lids,
you'll see at last the magnificent hall,
relish the twanging chords

and laughter of warriors like you
gathered to recite lines
over a banquet, to hear
music only a god could play.

Walk about gingerly, and spot
a man sprawled out in the sun,
his face dusted with pollen,
looking calmly at the sky.

Bees crawl all over his cheeks,
and from afar you'd swear
he's wearing a mask of gold (and
black, to remind you of despair).

His honeyed tongue greets you;
he's lord of the wondrous manor.
Stingless bees loved him, taught him
harmony and beauty. Now is your chance for valor.

ABOUT THE AUTHOR

NED CONDINI, writer, translator, and literary critic, was born in Turin, Northern Italy, and moved to the United States in 1976. An American citizen, he is the author of a novel, *Eldorado*, published in Verona, Italy, in 1991. An English teacher at Westwood, New Jersey, in 1986 he was the recipient of the PEN/Poggioli Award for translations of Mario Luzi. His short stories and poems have appeared in *The Mississippi Review, Prairie Schooner, The Partisan Review, Mid-American Review, Negative Capability, Italian Americana, The Paterson Review,* and the *BBC* of London. In May 1993, Condini's collection of poems, *Rimbaud in Umbria,* was published by Multigraf, Venice, Italy. In 1994, he won first prize in the *Abiko Literary Press* fiction contest (Abiko, Japan), and, in 1995, the Gozzano Award (Novara, Italy).